The Book on Money Management for Kids

A Beginners Investing, Saving, and Finance book for Children

By Thomas Turner

TABLE OF CONTENTS

Introduction

Finance is a topic that even adults shy away from. In a culture like ours where talking about money is considered almost impolite, it is difficult to dispel further the aura of mystery people have built around finance.

On the surface, financial concepts seem too complex to be comprehensible. However, it is just a layering of multiple simple concepts. Once you take the time to explore the topic, it starts becoming interesting.

Proper money management is the only way to get control or freedom. It is a path to hope, possibility, and a brighter future. It is a path to creating the life you want. It is the only way to keep your money from diminishing over time.

With understanding money, the first thing you get is safety. It helps to let go of some of the worries around cash. Anyone can learn money. But the earlier you know about it, the more advantageous it can prove to be. Children assimilate an incredible amount of information and use it to make sense of the world. If they are taught to understand money at that age, they would have a positive approach to finance.

This book aims to introduce financial topics as not just concepts but also as implementable habits. Having healthy financial habits is a step towards financial literacy. If you are interested in money—how to save it, how to invest it, and how to make more of it—then this is the book for you!

The earlier you start investing your money, the more money you can make! Time is one of the most powerful tools for building wealth, and as a kid, you have something that most grown-ups don't time! Learning about money and investing is not only beneficial to you, but it can also be helpful to the adults in your life. So, have fun learning together!

Just keep in mind that you should never invest your money without prior adult approval and supervision. I am conscious that I should not burden children at a young age. At the same time, it would be nice for them to know the basic money concepts.

Are they going to become money smart after reading the book? No. It is to get them to know the basics and influence their money behavior. That said, children subconsciously learn by observing the parent's money habits. So, parents, too, need to follow these concepts!

I hope that reading this book is your first step on an exciting journey that you can benefit from for the rest of your life.
Enjoy!

DEDICATION

**This book is dedicated to my Father
Ulester Mahoney Sr.**

ACKNOWLEDGMENTS

I WOULD LIKE TO ACKNOWLEDGE ALL THE HARD WORK OF THE MEN AND WOMEN OF THE UNITED STATES MILITARY, WHO RISK THEIR LIVES ON A DAILY BASIS, TO MAKE THE WORLD A SAFER PLACE.

Disclaimer Notice

This book was written as a guide and for information, educational and entertainment purposes only. No warranties of any kind are expressed or implied.

Readers acknowledge that the author is not engaging in the rendering of legal, financial, medical or professional advice, and the information in this book is not meant to take the place of any professional advice. If advice is needed in any of these fields, you are advised to seek the services of a professional.

While the author has attempted to make the information in this book as accurate as possible, no guarantee is given as to the accuracy or currency of any individual item. Laws and procedures related to business, health and well being are constantly changing.

Therefore, in no event shall the author of this book be liable for any special, indirect, or consequential damages or any damages whatsoever in connection with the use of the information herein provided.

Chapter One: Saving vs Spending: Money Management For Kids

What is money? Money Is a Tool

First, you must understand that money is just a tool. Money is a tool in the same way a hammer is a tool. The hammer is simply a hammer. It has no feelings or thoughts about what you do with it. It doesn't know you neither conspires against you. Yet, people get incredibly emotional with money. They project a lot onto it.

So, step one, drop all the emotional baggage you have attached to money—it is just a tool.
Simply put, money is stored goods and services. It is potential energy waiting to be released. It also has power because it is your decision when and how it gets released.

Money also represents the exchange of goods and services. It is a massive improvement from thousands of years ago when bartering was how the value was transferred from a farmer to a builder: if you give me a few chickens, I will build something for you in exchange.

The collective idea of money grew out of those experiences. It went from a direct trade of goods and services into exchanging rocks, gold, silver, and salt. These symbols were easier to transport and reach an agreement with.

Just like with any tool, money has a learning curve. If you practice diligently over time, you can master the tool. As a kid, you could bang a hammer to make a birdhouse. But if you stay with it, you can get to the point where you can build fine cabinetry or even a real house.

It is the same with money. With enough practice, you can master money.

There are different types of money depending on what country you live in. But all money has one thing in common. It allows you to use the currency to buy other items such as food, toys, clothing, and shelter. Money puts a price or value on the cost of each item that people or companies are supplying to others. Money has been around in some fashion for hundreds of years.

When you think about it, you need money for almost everything. If you want to eat, you need money. If you want new clothes, you need money. If you want to live in a nice house, you need money. Money should not be your ultimate goal, but it should be something you learn to master so that you can spend more time doing things you love.

Life is about doing things you enjoy and have a passion for. Life is about spending time with loved ones. Do not let time pass you by. Decide to control your current and future finances by learning the key elements of money management. Ignorance can be costly, so educate yourself and live the life you are meant to live.

Saving vs. Spending

For some children, managing money is a complex process. They receive their little income every two weeks or monthly, but they have nothing left by the end of the month.

Learning to save and spend less requires planning and discipline. If you have trouble having discipline with your spending habits, you will need to follow the simple rule of paying yourself first. By paying yourself first and sticking to a specific amount or minimum percentage of what you receive each month, and put it in a separate savings account, you will eliminate spending all of your money. It is one of the most effective ways to save money.

Having money saved will allow you to be prepared for the future, and since the future is never certain, it is better to have a little extra saved.

When you save money, money grows. It's like planting an orange tree. You paid for the tree one time, but once it starts giving you oranges, it will continue to do so as long as you take care of it. Money is often like that orange tree.

When you spend, you never recover the money you spend. If you buy oranges at the supermarket, you will get what you paid for, but you have to go to the supermarket and buy more if you want more oranges. It means you have to go and work more to pay for more oranges.

Decide to plant more orange trees, so you don't have to go to the supermarket to buy more oranges. Planting an orange tree is similar to planting a money tree, but in this case, saving and earning from the money you have saved will be your money tree. Use coupons to save money

You can't coupon without coupons, right? The first step in your couponing journey is to start building up a collection of coupons. It is best to clip or print coupons as they become ready when a deal comes up. The two most common sources of coupons are newspapers and the internet.

Newspapers

You can either subscribe to a newspaper that includes coupon inserts or buy individual papers depending on their inserts for the week. How many pieces should you buy? My suggestion is two to four sets of inserts each week. Start with purchasing two papers as you get acclimated to couponing.

Once you get the routine down and streamline your process, you can add additional sets of inserts to maximize the amount of product you can buy. You can also swap coupons with friends. Trade coupons that you know you won't use with ones that they don't need.

Online Coupons

Printing coupons online is becoming more popular than clipping newspaper inserts. The number of coupons that are available online is simply staggering. To find coupons online, check out these popular websites: www.coupons.com, www.redplum.com, www.smartsource.com, www.commonkindness.com, and www.target.com.

Also, you can often find coupons on the Facebook page for your favorite product, websites for your favorite stores, and websites for your favorite brands. It pays to spend fifteen minutes a few times a week searching online for coupons to print.

To save money using coupons, you need to stock up on items on sale while buying a few "needed" items. To save serious money using coupons, you buy what is on sale and as much of it as possible. If you stock up on items when they are at their lowest prices and do this consistently week after week, you will soon have a well-stocked pantry and more cash in your wallet. As your stockpile grows, both your list of needed items will get smaller and smaller.

Productive spending

While it is super important to save, there are times when you spend some of your savings. You may want to earn more money, too. You might have the idea to start a lawn mowing business, for example. So you decide to use some of your savings to buy a used lawnmower in good condition.

The lawnmower is an example of productive spending. You are spending on something that will help you make money. For a business, this is called capital investment.

Another example is if you decide to learn more about investing.

First, you go to the library to use the free resources available online and offline.

Second, you decide to buy your copy of a book about investing since you have used up your library's amount of time to let you keep the book checked out. Or the book might not be available through your library.

If using the book will help you increase the amount of money you make on your investments, it is another example of productive spending.

Need Vs. Want?

Did you know that needing and wanting are not the same thing?

Let us explore the difference. Suppose you live in a freezing state such as Montana during the winter. If you don't stay warm, you could freeze to death. In this case, having a warm coat is a need. But having three different expensive parkas goes beyond your basic need for warmth. It's a want.

A need can be different for different people. If you live in Florida, you certainly don't need a parka, but you may need an air conditioner. Each time you spend your money, think about whether the item is a need or a want.

In lots of families, the parent(s) or guardian(s) pay for the needs of everyone in the family. But when it comes to your wants, they may tell you to pay for them using your allowance, gifts, and earnings.

One easy way to save money is to limit your spending on wants. After all, having one pair of cool sneakers may be a need, but having two or three isn't. Economists have a fancy word for this – they call it utility. The utility of the first pair of sneakers is high, but it goes down quickly for that second pair and even more so for a third pair.

Usually, the best way to decide if you want to spend your money on something is to wait. To put this in action, suppose you want to buy a video game. Instead of running out and getting it, wait a month. If you still really, really want to buy the video game at the end of a month, then you know it's important to you.

You might want to write down each of the things you wanted to buy that month. At the end of the month, you can review your list. Maybe there is something you still want to buy. On the other hand, you might be glad your money is still in your account!

Families spent money depending on the needs of each person in the family. Basic food, education, housing safety, and saving for the future are all needs. If there is enough money left after spending on the needs, families think about spending on wants. Ask your mother if this is the reason she did not let you buy something you wanted? Ask her what she did with the money instead?

Keeping track of expenses

Most people earn money by working for themselves or someone else. A family may have one or more members with incomes. A family spends and saves depending on incomes, the needs, and the expenses it has to make. A budget is a plan of action for this. These are the scenes that may occur in most families.

Income equals expenses

There is no money left for saving or for being given to others as loans. Taking care of any unforeseen expense will make the situation difficult for this family.

Income is less than the expense

This is not the best situation for a family to be in. this means the family has to borrow to match the expenses. Loans have to be returned within a short period along with interest. The family has to reduce expenses to ensure that income is closer to the expenses. In extreme cases, if they do not get a loan, they will have to sell an asset like TV to get the money.

Income is more than the expense

The extra money left after all the expenses can be saved in many ways or invested in plans that make your money grow. It is a situation that all of us aim for. The better the income, the more we can spend on needs and save for the future.

Budgeting

A budget is a way to keep track of the money you earn, the money you spend, and the money you save over some time. The information in your budget is crucial because it helps you understand how your money is being used and how much you have to spend or save.

Expenses are of different kinds-short term and long-term. The family has to keep the money for everyday expenses and monthly expenses. Money should also be set aside for yearly expenses. A family budget is a plan for your family's money.

To create your budget, you need details. In your budget, list all the sources of your income. Then list all of your expenses. Donations should be listed as well.

A budget is made as a guide to help manage your income in the best way possible. Savings are what is left after you subtract your expenses and donations from your income.

Let us say you earn $15 per week. How will you divide it into savings and spending?

It will depend on what you are responsible for paying. You might have to buy your mobile phone apps, e-books, video apps, and school snacks. This is where your budget will come in handy. Below is a weekly budget example for 12-year-old Sarah:

Income: Allowance $15.00

Expenses

- School snacks -5.00
- Weekly apps -2.00
- Weekly e-books -2.00
- Donation -1.00
- Savings 5.00

It means Sarah will be saving $5 a week.

Now it is time to do your budget. Remember to pay yourself first, and put the savings in an account or investment right away to not spend the money.

A budget does not have to be something that is all that complicated. It is just a plan and a breakdown of how you will spend your earnings.

You can start by listing the amount of money you will get each month and the sources from where it might come. These include allowance money, money from working, and even birthday money.

Once you know how much money you will be getting in during the month, you will plan out how much you can spend each month without going into debt.

You might spend your money on toys, clothes, entertainment, gifts, savings, and anything else that might come up throughout the month.

Having a budget in place can be a great way to help you avoid going into debt. When you are not sure how much money you are spending each month, it can be challenging to know how to keep track of your budget. Just by listing out the things you need to pay for each month and subtracting them from the amount of money you make each month to know what is left for you to spend.

When you are coming up with a budget, it is good to keep in mind that you do not have to give up everything you currently enjoy. It is okay to go out to the movies on occasion with some friends or splurge on some new shoes that you want. The important thing is to recognize that you must pay off your debts first, deal with your savings, and then use the money left over at the end of the month to pay for some of the extras.

You must also realize that you might not be able to afford things right when you want to. Just because you have the right amount of money for the thing you want right away does not mean that you should splurge on it right then. If you need to put money in savings or have other needs to meet with the money, it is best to save up a little bit until you can afford it better.

There are a few steps that you should keep in mind when setting up your budget. The first thing you should do is go around and gather all of the receipts you can for items you have recently purchased.

These can include receipts for clothes, toys, and anything else that you have spent money on. All of these papers are meant to help you see where you are spending your money, spending it wisely, and giving you a basis for spending less if you are going over your budget amount.

Next, you should make sure to record all of the income sources that you have. For a young child, this will be their allowance. Record this amount down so you have a basis for money that you can spend. The third thing you should do is write down all of the things you have to spend your money on. It is always advisable to make a list of the items you intend to buy. Make a rough estimation of the cost of the things too.

It is essential to learn how to budget when you are young because it is a tool that you will have to use for the rest of your life. You might find through life that you are spending more than your budget allows, and you can use some of these suggestions to get back on track and spend within your means. It means that you might have to get rid of some of the extras in your life or find new ways to make some money. Increasing your income and decreasing your spending are the two best ways to keep your budget on track and take some hard work to accomplish.

How can I make money as a kid?

Allowance

For many kids, an allowance is their only source of money or at least a big part of it.

So, what exactly is an allowance?

An allowance is a regular payment of money from your parent(s) or guardian(s). Deciding the basis for an allowance, what you have to do to earn it, is up to the adults in the family.

Some families require you to do chores around the house for an allowance. You may receive a set amount of money each week for doing things like washing the dishes, taking out the garbage, mowing the lawn, and other chores.

If you don't do your chores a particular week, you probably won't get your allowance for that week. Other families don't require you to do chores for an allowance. They feel that everyone in a family should contribute to the family without getting paid for their efforts.

In this situation, the adults in the family give an allowance to spend money to learn the value of having money. Neither way of determining an allocation is better than the other. It's simply family preference.

The allowance is up to your parent(s) or guardian(s) as it needs to fit their budget. It will also likely reflect your age. Most adults will increase your allowance as you get older because your needs will increase and because (hopefully) you have demonstrated that you are responsible with your allowance.

Whether you work hard for it or simply part of a family that gives allowances, take care of the money you get. Please keep it in a safe place, so you don't lose it. And use a budget to determine what you will do with it.

Gifts

Ah, yes, there is another way you can get money. It might be your birthday, a holiday, or even when your grandparent visits. These are all times when you may receive a gift of money.

So, what should you do with monetary gifts (gifts of money) that you receive? The first thing is to make sure to write a thank-you note to the giver! After saying thanks, this is another source of money that you need to manage carefully. As with an allowance or money you earn from working outside the home, keep it in a safe place, so you don't lose it. You might also put gift money into your savings right away.

Pet sitting

This is usually a one-off job – people will want you to feed, groom and walk their pets while they're away on holiday. People are often pretty generous with the final pay check, generally around $3-10 each day.

You can offer up these services to your friends & neighbors when you know they're going away and will need someone to look after their pet. Make sure to choose wisely with regards to which animals you agree to look after.

Dog Walking

The amount of money you earn from dog walking can vary a lot. For example, if you find a couple of people who want you to take their dog out daily (maybe because they work until late or something like that), then that's great, and you can earn plenty of money. However, if you only walk dogs when people go on holiday (generally once or twice a year), you won't make all that much.

Also, make sure you tell people what you are willing to do – walking someone's pet gerbil, though strange, is acceptable. But you might want to think twice before walking zebras, for example.

Adventures in Babysitting

Another of the classics. I know many people who regularly make up to $40 a week just by sitting in someone's house while the parents are out and playing on their iPhones.

This is also an excellent time to get a bit of homework done, freeing up other times when you're at home to do more fun things.

Ensure you bring plenty of things to keep you entertained, as babysitting can get boring if you don't. Please don't rely on the TV working as it inevitably won't, and Wi-Fi will be pretty hard to connect to. Your best option is to bring a good book (or your Kindle with a few books on it).

Before the parents leave, make sure to ask them for an emergency contact number, where any medical supplies are (i.e., plasters), and if any of the children have any medical conditions.

Delivering/Handing out brochures

A big part of many businesses' marketing campaigns is handing out brochures, discount coupons, or anything else that they can use to gain customers. However, delivering these can take quite a while, with the time it takes to go around a village posting brochures or standing in a busy place giving them to passers-by.

Many of these companies would love for someone else to give them out, but they don't realize what options they have available. Just start contacting local businesses by email or by phone and offering to do this for them (if you can get several interested, you might be able to deliver them all at once).

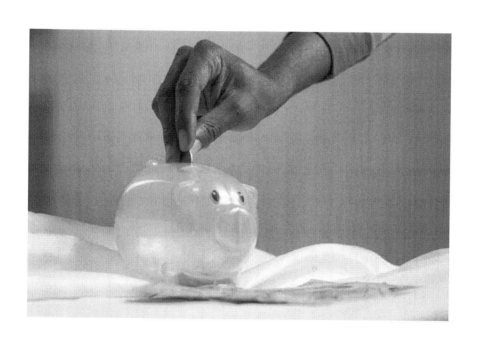

Chapter Two:
How To Save
Money As A Kid

Have you ever heard the saying "Pay yourself first?" Maybe you haven't yet. But it's a great money rule. It means to have a specified amount of the money you earn each week set aside to save. As soon as you get paid, that amount immediately goes into your savings.

So, why is paying yourself first such a great money rule? Well, who cares the most about your money and what it can do for you?

YOU DO!

It only makes sense to choose to save money now to give you more choices in the future. Let us say you want a bike, but you don't have enough money to buy one. You will need to save to purchase the bike. You look at the money you have saved and the money you get each week. You do the math and find out that it will take you eight weeks of saving all the money you get to buy the bike. So, each week you put your money in your cash box or personal safe. You pay yourself first.

At the same time, your best friend decides to save for a bike as well. But at the end of the first week, your friend spends all of that week's money on candy and ice cream. The following week your friend spends all his money on a book of stickers that he just had to have. The third week, your friend spends his weekly money plus dips into his savings to buy a video game.

While you continue to save each week, your friend continues to spend. At the end of eight weeks, you buy your bike. But your friend, well, he cannot buy a bike because he doesn't have enough money.

Not only do you have the bike you wanted, but you also have the freedom to ride to the park or school, with parental permission if needed, of course.

Your friend, not so much. He has to rely on his parent(s) or guardian(s) for a ride, or he has to walk. Saving your money resulted in having more choices. Make saving one of your TOP priorities, and start saving NOW!

Why Should You Save Money When You Are So Young?

It's easier to save money when you have a specific goal in mind, but it can be challenging to save money simply for the sake of saving money. It takes the right kind of motivation to accomplish your goals in life, and saving money requires just as much motivation as the rest of your goals.

Be wise and realize that the effort you put into something now will reflect what you get out of it later.

Certain people might give you a rough time because they only see a tiny fraction of the picture. The picture begins to expand as you start making progress towards achieving your goals. You will begin to gain reassurance. You will realize that you did the right thing. Making money is only one part of the game.

You should dedicate just as much time and effort to saving your money as you commit to making money. Think of making money as drinking water and saving money as food. You need both to survive. How much you need will depend on the person and their plans, but everyone needs a little of both.

It can be challenging to see the importance of saving money when you are young, just like it can be challenging to see the importance of drinking water when you are only six years old. If you feel thirsty when you are six years old, you will drink flavored drinks with sugar in them. Later on, in life, you will realize it's healthier and better to drink water more often. Buying the wrong things instead of saving your money is like drinking something that ends up dehydrating you. It just doesn't make sense in the long run.

It's easy enough to understand the desire for making and spending money, but we seem to get lost and confused when it comes to saving it. Many people would panic if they stopped making money, but they seem to be perfectly carefree with the idea of not saving it. Sometimes we have to learn the hard way.

Some of us might not see the importance of saving money until the flow of cash stops. Don't make that mistake. Don't wait until something dramatic happens before you finally open your eyes to the importance of saving money. You need to have just as much respect for saving money as you do for making money.

Don't be negative about saving money. Have a positive outlook on your life and see each dollar that you save as another step closer to reaching your goals, even if you don't have any financial goals as of right now. There are so many different reasons to save money, and you never know what you might need the extra cash for in the future. It's always good to save more than what you think you will need.

Where can I save my money?

Real bank or Piggybank

Where should you keep the money you are saving? While you could keep it in your house somewhere safe such as your wallet, a piggy bank, or with your parents, you might also choose to keep some of it in the bank.

Piggy Banks are not always piggies. They can be elephants, pirate ships, toy houses, or even pretend bars of gold. So why are they called piggy banks? The word 'piggy' comes from a brownish-red clay called 'pygg' used in the Middle Ages in Britain to make pots. Money was kept safe in pots made from pygg clay, and the words pygg and pig got mixed up, and the name stuck.

Modern piggy banks have rubber bungs to be emptied, but the only way to get the money out was smash the pot in the olden days.

Today, there are many types of the money box, including skeletal hands emerging from money coffins, combination safes, and fake bars of gold, but they all have the same purpose: to store money safely and stop children from spending as soon as they get it. Combination locks are helpful to prevent parents, big sisters, or little brothers from dipping their hands in for some loose change.

Girl saving up coins in to the piggy bank

Banking and You

Piggy banks or money boxes are for keeping coins and the occasional folded banknote, but if you are serious about your finances, you need to have a bank account. Banks are very keen to offer junior or starter accounts to children.

They reckon that you are very likely to keep it there for the rest of your life once you have an account with them. Ask your parents or even grandparents how long they had their account at the same bank probably well before you were born. They may have a joint account, too, to access money from the same account.

Most children don't need a checking account at the bank until they have a job but what you can open at the bank is a savings account. There are many kinds of savings accounts, but all of them give you interest in the money you put into your account. Just as you 'pay' interest if you owe money, the bank pays you interest if you have a savings account.

Interest is the money the bank pays you for the right to use your money. Banks make money by lending your money to other people or organizations, even to other banks. As well as the fees it charges, the bank receives higher interest from lending out your money than it gives back to you. The bank, therefore, makes a profit, but since it pays you interest, you make a profit too.

Saving Money, and Thinking About The Future

There is always the possibility that you might change your mind about certain things in the future. Things change, people change, and plans change. You might still live at home, or you might move out. You might end up buying an expensive house, or you might end up getting a good deal on a small condo. You might be able to get around without a car for now, but you might end up needing one in another five years.

We have our goals for the future, but we can't always predict the obstacles that we will have to face. It's good to live in the present moment, but we need to think about the future regarding how we choose to spend our money. Don't think that ten years is too far away when you think about saving money.

If it takes you years and years to save enough money for something that's important, ten years might not be so far away after all. You can't always assume that you will just fall into a ton of money in the future somehow. You can start making things happen now by saving money as you think about your future. Give yourself a break later on by saving money now.

Don't be too hard on yourself, but don't go so easy on yourself either. It's alright to spend more money than you would have liked occasionally. Don't drive yourself crazy by never allowing yourself to buy something that you want. Saving money not only requires time but practice.
As you practice thinking about all of the money that you will need in the future, you will slip deeper into the habit of saving your money in the present.

Debt

When discussing money and saving, the topic of debt is likely to pop up.
Why is that? What is debt anyway?
Debt is when you spend more money than you have. It means you borrowed money from another person or another company, and you'll need to pay them back.

When you're in debt, you give up some of your money freedom. This means your money isn't all yours anymore. When you earn an extra dollar, some or all of that dollar has to go the person or company you owe money to.

Being in debt is a worry. You may worry about how you will earn enough to pay the person or company you owe. You may even begin to resent that person or company, even though it was you who decided to borrow money.

You want to avoid debt.

Today, it seems most adults are in some kind of debt. According to the Federal Reserve's latest numbers, the average household in the United States owes about $137,000. Pretty sad that the average household is in debt for that much!

One way people get into debt is by using credit cards. Studies show that when people use credit cards, they don't have the same "pain" sensation when using cash. So, the tendency is to spend more with credit cards.

Being aware of this should help you avoid debt. On the flip side, it may sometimes be useful to borrow money for a big purchase such as a house that will usually (but not always) increase in value. A house is called an appreciating asset. But most debt is used to buy things that go down in value. This is how people get into trouble with debt. A new car, for example, goes down in value by 33% the minute the new owner drives it out of the car dealer's lot. The car is called a depreciating asset.

Chapter Three: How To Open Your First Bank Account

What should your first account be?

Let's go over the different options to help you decide.

Option One:

Your parent(s) or guardian(s) agree to be your bank. They might also agree to pay you interest on your savings. And, because they care for you, they may pay you more interest than you would receive elsewhere.

We discussed what interest is in the previous chapter.

Option Two:

You save your money in a real bank. Many banks have special accounts for kids and teens. These accounts may not require a minimum money deposit, such as required for adults. These accounts may also have a higher interest rate than accounts for adults. Also, these accounts may have other benefits, such as gift certificates.

Option Three:

You put your savings in an account with an investment company such as Schwab, Fidelity, or Vanguard, to name just a few. Many of these companies also offer special accounts for kids and teens. They may also provide other benefits.

How to Choose the Best Bank Accounts for Kids? Bank accounts for the kids had opened new opportunity doors for banks.

These accounts do more than just save the amount of money for the kids. It encourages savings among their age, spreading the word of its importance, what financial responsibility is, what independence of spending your money feels like, and most importantly, how to manage your expenditures.

These education requirements are not taught in any books but can be only taught with experience. Almost every bank offers this type of service today. How do we differentiate those accounts and decide on the best or ideal as per our needs and wants?

To answer the above question, we need to know what type of bank account we want. There are many types of bank accounts offered to kids these days. Two of the most common ones are interest-earning saving accounts and joint checking accounts. Both have their features and serves its' own unique purpose.

Once we have chosen the type of banking account we wish to open up, we have various options as many banks would be offering that particular type of account. It is the time when we compare between those similar accounts and choose the best option.

For choosing the best option, parents must help you to look for the nearest banks to your home so their children can enjoy the convenience of depositing or withdrawing their own money at their flexible time. Considering those areas, choose the banks with no maintenance fees, as having maintenance fees can discourage you from saving; you would rather choose your piggy bank to save in that sense.

The third factor to consider is that the interest-earning potential. Choose the banks that offer more interest compounded regularly to your savings; hence this will encourage you to save more. Your mum or dad can help you in making such choices. The fourth factor to consider is choosing the bank with no transaction fees charged but offers a minimum balance.

Having a minimum balance in your account is necessary because you learn to manage your spending and that within a certain range. With this option, you will learn to limit your excessive spending and differentiate between what you need and what you desire to have.

Different Types of Kids Bank Accounts

Traditionally, the banking services were targeted to adults only, as since they earn money, they will be willing to save it. However, the recent events had changed its course about the whole idea of the banking served: which served 'anyone' who is willing to save or manage their expenditures.

For a particular target, banking services offered are different as it needs to be customized as per the needs and wants of that target only. Hence, kids are provided with varying accounts of banking than others. The types of banking accounts offered are education savings account, interest-earning savings account, joint checking accounts, and custodial accounts. Each of these serves a different purpose to meet all the needs and wants of those kids.

Education savings account sells the ideology to save for bearing primary, secondary, or college expenses. These are generally set up for an individual who is under eighteen by a family member. It can take the form of a brokerage fund or mutual fund as well. However, all such accounts are non-deductible and tax-free.

Interest-earning savings accounts are offered in most banks that are specially designed for children. Such accounts serve to educate children on the importance of saving and giving them the idea of financial responsibility. In the process of encouraging more kids to save and take on this responsibility, no penalty fees are charged. Kids can easily deposit their money and learn to save their own money, earning interest each year in a compounding method.

However, the policy for the requirement of the minimum balance differs from bank to bank. Hence, when opening a bank account, it is the responsibility of the parents to explain this matter to the kids well. Joint checking accounts are those accounts where the kid's account is joined with the parents' account.

So, parents will get the idea of how their child is spending the money and is saving. With that, they will have more control over their kid's expenses and teach them the better way to save. This control comes with the option of withdrawal limit where parents decide how much their child can spend only for a particular time. However, no fees are charged for such accounts.

Custodial accounts are those accounts where a specified amount of money is transferred to the account of the person who holds the custody of their children. The person who holds the custody plays the role of parents, with which the custodian manages the kids' expenses.

Benefits of Kids Banking

Saving accounts are essential for everyone. They are important for different people for different reasons. Banking for kids gives them a secure future and an understanding of how to manage money. Saving accounts are important for a nation because it provides a bank with an investment opportunity, thus helping the economy. The American economy is improving - slowly. After the recent recession, there has never been a more important time to look into the rewards of kids banking.

The benefits of kids banking in the USA today are enormous. Putting money into the bank means a kid will go through college without any financial worries. They may be able to own their first car without having to worry about securing finance for it. Most importantly, they will learn the value of saving. Having money to save gives a person a sense of responsibility and maturity.

Saving from an early age instills a habit that will be hard for you to break. It will make you wiser and more diligent. More than just going some way to securing your future, your bank will teach you basic finance concepts. Basic finance is something even a significant number of business owners fail to understand.

It was estimated that a glaring amount of independently ran stores closed simply because the owners failed to understand terms such as 'positive equity.' In a nation where understanding the economy is becoming increasingly important, kids' banking benefits far outweigh the negatives.

Understanding the basics of how an economy works will help to shape their sense of money management. In a world of celebrity exposure, where money often seems like no object to the USA's mega-stars, the bank instills a sense of realism and perspective and doesn't encourage a distortion of the principles and value of money.

There has never been a better time for you to invest in kids banking in terms of the USA's economic performance. The inflation rates are down at the moment in the USA, with the current inflation rate being just 1.2% - the lowest for three years. Owing to the decrease in inflation rates now is as good a time as ever to invest in kids banking. When inflation is down, and interest rates are up, saving proves invaluable.

Therefore, as well as saving for a more secure future, a kids bank also makes money. Ultimately, kids banking is becoming more and more a necessity in a world controlled by fluctuations in our economy. Recognizing this, banks add various benefits to the kids bank account, such as education and accident cover. Saving and managing money will inevitably become an important part of a child's life, so it is essential to teach them the value of saving.

Chapter Four: Getting Your First Credit Card

Credit cards are often used today, that it's hard to believe they were not in existence before the 1950s. Suppose you want to buy something and you don't have cash for it. A credit card allows you to pay for something today without spending cash on getting it. It is not free money. Its simply a way for you to extend the time you have to pay something back to the bank that loaned you the money on the card.

Credit cards are plastic cards that have an account number on them. When you pay for something, the magnetic strip on the back is scanned so that the merchant can get the information to give you a receipt for your purchase.

Newer credit cards have a magnetic chip on them that a scanner can read. These magnetic chips have better security features and are intended to limit credit card fraud.

You are using the credit card to pay using the credit limit that a particular bank has issued. In other words, you are using the banks' money. It is real money that the bank has.

You promise to pay this money back to the bank every time you use the card. Almost all merchants accept different credit cards, so you can use a credit card to buy just about anything, including dinner out, video games, or clothing.

If you use credit cards wisely, it helps you to establish a credit profile. If you have good credit, then its easier to make larger purchases in the future that may require a loan, such as when you buy a car or a house.

How old do you have to be to own your credit card? In the United States, you have to be at least 18 years old to get your credit card. To qualify, you have to be earning money and have a steady amount of income. When you apply for a credit card, the banks want to know you can pay the money back; otherwise, you won't be a good credit risk.

A regular allowance that you get from your parents isn't seen as income by the bank. You would need to show that you have a job and are earning a regular paycheck. When you apply for your very first credit card, there are just a few potential options until you establish a credit history. You can look for a credit card designed specifically for students or a department store credit card. It is usually easier to apply for these types of cards.

Another way is to get a secured credit card. This type of card is slightly different since you have to put in a deposit before getting the card. The deposit is a portion of your credit limit, so if you default on the card, the bank can take your money.

It's a way for the bank to minimize its risk since you do not have a credit history yet.

If you are under 18 years old, an adult like your mum or dad can make you an authorized user on one of their credit cards. You will have a credit card that you can use, but they will be responsible for making the payments. Another way to use a credit card is to get a prepaid card. It looks like a credit card, but it isn't a true credit card. That's because you have to pay it in advance. In other words, you would pay $50 on a prepaid card ahead of time; then, you can use it as a credit card to pay for a $6 coffee drink. This type of card doesn't help you establish a credit history, but it is still convenient.

Using a credit card

There are at least four different ways to use credit cards to pay for something or get cash.

Pay in person

When you are in a store, and you want to buy something, you present your credit card to the cashier to pay for the purchase. The magnetic strip on the backside of the card is run through a terminal that verifies the purchase.

Sometimes, if the terminal is not working or is not allowed to charge any more on that card, your purchase will be approved.

Pay over the phone or internet.

If you buy something by using your phone or buying it on the internet, you will have to provide specific information so that the merchant can verify you and your credit card. You will be asked to give your account number, the month, and the year that the card expires. You will need to provide your full name and address too. There is a three-digit security number on the back of the card you may be asked to supply.

Get cash at an ATM

You can sometimes use your credit card to get cash from an Automated Teller Machine or ATM. There is a limit to the amount o cash you can get based on your credit limit and credit history. There are sometimes very high fees for this service.

Use a special check issued by the credit card company

Sometimes credit cards will issue checks in the mail.

You can use these checks to deposit an amount from your credit limit into your bank account. Once again, the fees for the service are usually high.

Credit cards mean debt

Unless you pay off your credit card bills every month, you will be in debt. You owe the money to the banks that issued you your credit card. When you receive the invoice, it will show the interest rate you are paying.

It will also give you the option of sending in minimum payment. The statement will provide you the total amount that you owe.

The bank that issued you the card makes its money on the interest rate and fees charged to you. Many people pay the minimum amounts on their credit card bills, and they have "revolving debt." They continue to pay interest on the purchases they already made, and then they buy more things and owe interest to the new stuff they purchased as well. A credit card doesn't have a specific end date when it must be completely paid off, so the interest is just charged every month until you pay off the bill in full.

Credit card fees

Credit cards have many different types of fees. There may be fees charged for late payments, going over your credit limit, and an annual fee simply for the right to use the card.

Use credit card responsibly

Paying by credit card isn't free money. Although the bank that issues the credit card initially pays for your purchase, you will need to make payments and pay interest and fees until the purchase has been completely paid off.

Chapter Five:
How To Get
Started Investing
Your Money

Investing is when you put money aside, often with an investment company, and expect to get more money in return. You want to see your money grow.

It's a good idea to have a goal for your investments. For example, you might want to save for college. The famous investor Warren Buffet says investing is "the process of laying out money now to receive more money in the future."

Some of the ways you can invest your money include certificates of deposit, bonds, stocks, and real estate. We will talk about each of these investments in the following paragraphs.

If you ever receive money and it's too much to fit into your piggy bank or money box, you need to decide what to do with it. You could spend some of it. You could save some of it. You could put some of it in a bank. You could give some away to a charity, or you could 'invest' some of it.

Investing money is not something children usually think about, but there are many ways that your money can make more money if you put it in the right place.

Certificates of deposits

First on the investment list are certificates of deposit.

But what is that?

A certificate of deposit is money you deposit with a bank for a specific amount of time.

When you make this deposit, you agree you will keep the money in the bank for a certain amount of time. Sometimes, the bank will agree to let you take your money out early (before the specified time) if you pay an early withdrawal penalty.

It is very different than a checking account or savings account, where you can get your money back when you want. So, when thinking about getting a certificate of deposit, be sure you won't need your money any time soon.

Generally, the certificate of deposit can be for any period from one month to five or more years. When that period is up, you get back the original amount of money you deposited along with interest on the deposit.

Because you agree to let the bank have your money for some time in a certificate of deposit, you will usually be paid a higher interest rate than on a checking account or savings account. A certificate of deposit is also called a CD.

Stocks

Next up on the investment list are stocks. What are stocks? A stock is a small piece of ownership in a company. There are two ways to make money from owning stock:

First, the company may pay stock owners a portion of its yearly profits. Those payments are called dividends.

Second, the company may increase in value. This means your stock will increase in value. If this happens, you could sell the stock for more money than you paid. The profits from selling your stock are called capital gains. There are two ways that you can buy stocks – individual stocks and stock funds.

Individual Stocks

You can buy the stock of an individual company. But there are risks to owning the stock of only one company, even if you research the company carefully. For example, if something bad happens to the economy, the stock of the one company you own may go down more than the stocks of other companies.

Stock Funds

To be safer, you might decide to invest in a stock fund. In a stock fund, you and other investors pool your money and buy stocks (or shares) in several companies. Owning the stocks of many companies is called diversification. It is a critical way to reduce risk.

Two of the most popular types of funds you can buy are exchanging traded funds and mutual funds. In an exchange-traded fund, the fund manager is usually only allowed to buy the stocks of companies in a particular stock index. An example of a stock index is the Dow Jones Industrial Average, also known as the Dow. The Dow contains 30 large companies such as Apple, Walt Disney, McDonald's, and Coca-Cola.

In a mutual fund, the fund manager is usually allowed to buy the stocks that he or she thinks are better than other stocks.

Both types of funds charge you a small amount for management expenses. These expenses are usually a bit lower for an exchange-traded fund.

If you are a beginner at stock investing, you should get advice from your parent(s) or guardian(s). Never invest your money in something that you don't understand. Let's say that again. Never invest your money in something that you don't understand. Get educated so that you can be an intelligent investor!

Why does a company sell stock?

Most of the time, they sell their stock to raise money for expansion. If they sell the stock, then they do not need to take a loan out and pay interest. The funds received after selling stock are used to do things like hiring new employees or building.

What is the stock exchange?

The place where stocks are bought and sold is referred to as a stock exchange. There are many stock exchanges globally, including two of the largest exchanges in the United States; the NASDAQ and the New York stock exchange are located in New York City.

Your sandwich shop

Suppose you own a very successful sandwich shop that everybody loved, and you made a ton of money.

Each year your sandwich shop has made approximately $80,000, and you decide to open nine other shops throughout the country.

With ten shops, you would now be making an $800,000 profit. But you realize it would cost you a lot of money to open the other nine shops. Obtaining a loan from a bank would be one option, and another option would be selling stock in your business.

So after thinking about these options, you decide to sell stock and sold 50% of your company to people with shares of stock. It provided you with the funds needed to open the other nine shops.

At years end, you might reward your investors with 50% of the profits in the form of dividends. If all the new shops were as profitable as the original shop, they would receive $400,000 from you, which leaves you with $400,000.

Even though you did not make all of the money, you made more than you did when you only had one shop.

Why Invest in Stocks as a Kid?

Money, money, money, or maybe because you know that investing in stocks no matter your age will help you save and gain financial independence. Stock investing ensures you have a path to be comfortable in life no matter the difficulties you face with employment, economic hardships, and more. Plenty can happen from the time you are twelve to thirty, such as becoming a millionaire through invention.

You could publish a book. You might go to college, get a doctorate, and become a doctor. By investing in shares, you have a way to pay for whatever happens, without the concerns many people have.

For example, someone might hope for scholarships and end up paying $30,000 for a university education over fifteen years. Another person might be diagnosed with a disease, spend half a million in medical costs, and be healthy for the rest of their lives, but without significant savings. Stock investments allow you to contemplate the potential with minimal worries.

Investing in the stock market allows you to develop excellent money habits early. It will be easier to understand the nature of the volatility of the stock market as an adult. However, mistakes will not be so costly because you have less to lose in your younger years. You can make up tiny amounts throughout your life. As a child, your stock investment has more time to grow. You also have the magic of compounding interest to ensure your investments making money continue to do so.

Rather than being someone who lives from paycheck to paycheck, wondering whether health insurance is worth the cost or not given other expenses, you could know for sure that you have the money for necessities and then some. There are plenty of reasons you should invest in stocks as a kid beyond the apparent financial stability.

Inflation is an issue that can cause monetary losses. Economically, when prices rise, the purchase value of money decreases. Inflation can increase the price of a home, so the person selling the house gets more for its value. However, the one buying it has to use more money for the same product. In financial speak, inflation is a decrease in purchasing power for currency. In stock investment, your money can increase in value.

Real Estate

Next on the investment list is real estate, such as buildings or land. Real estate can be a good investment. The problem, though, is that real estate can be a challenging investment to make because it often requires a large amount of money.

Besides needing lots of money to buy into real estate, it usually takes longer to sell real estate when you want to get your cash out. Because you can't quickly get your money back, like with bonds and stocks, this type of investment is an illiquid investment.

Kids are not able to own real estate outright. Parents need to be on the title and sign the papers. However, they can name their children as beneficiaries to the property. It does not mean you can't start real estate investment once you are an adult and use it as an investment tool. However, real estate requires a lot of funds, and it can turn against you in the wrong economic situation. There is nothing wrong with having a diverse portfolio. It is best to start with stock investment as a kid and move up to other investments.

Bonds

Bonds are similar to loans. When you purchase a bond, you are lending your money to the Government or a company. While bonds might pay a higher interest rate than a bank account, they also come with additional risks.

Once you have thought about these options, discuss them with your parent(s) or guardian(s). They can help you choose one or more of these investments so that you can start investing NOW!

Compound interest - The most powerful force on earth

Compound interest is the interest you are paid on your savings and the interest you have earned from those savings kept in a bank account. The interest you are paid does not require that you work for it or do any additional tasks. The bank pays you this money for keeping your money in their bank account. It's that simple and very effective if consistently done over time.

How do you start getting paid compound interest?

Go to a bank and find out the most they pay in interest in their bank accounts and confirm that the claim is compounded on a monthly or daily basis. You do not want to get paid interest that is compounded quarterly or yearly because so many other banks compound interest monthly or even daily.

Once you find the bank that pays the highest interest rate and that compounds daily or monthly, ask the bank representative what requirements that account has in terms of minimum amounts to open and if any fees are associated with the account. Don't pay any fees. If you do, you will lose the benefit of compound interest. Always choose an account that has no fees, pays the highest interest rate, and that compounds interest monthly at the very least.

Your goal should be to make automatic deposits every month in a specific amount so that you can see your money grow and start seeing the effects of compound interest. You should see interest payments every month deposited into your account made by the bank. Getting paid interest is great but remember not to withdraw that interest so that you are paid interest on that interest on the following month. That is the cherry on top!

The sooner you start, the better. The younger you are, the more years you have to start receiving interest payments, and the more you can benefit from compound interest.

Small amounts can become larger over time using compound interest, so it does not matter if you start small. The key is to make consistent deposits every month and to get paid interest so that the compounding effects can exponentially grow. This is a simple, hands-off approach towards creating wealth that will truly amaze you once you start putting it into practice.

Take a Risk enjoy a Reward

There is risk in most investments, and you might end up in the future with less money than you had today. Some are riskier than others, but the more of a risk you are willing to take, the more money you might make.

Business people always take risks when investing money. Your family buys a piece of land, thinking it can be sold a few years later when the price goes up. Usually, the land cost goes up, but there have been times when the prices have come down. Selling land at such times results in a loss. The higher the risk, the chances are that there will be better returns. But the opposite is true- the more the returns, the higher the risk.

Taking risks in money matters is not illegal. But making money by doing things against the rules of the county is illegal. If a shopkeeper charges more than what is printed on the cover of the product, he makes illegal money.

A federal insured CD (certificate of deposit) from a bank is an example of an investment that is not too risky since the bank pays you a percentage over some time. Even if it goes out of business, your money should be insured by the Federal Government. While this sounds like a great idea, CDs only pay a low percent each year, which is not a great investment return.

Investing in the stock of a new technology company would be a riskier example of investment. Your money might go up a lot over the next few years if the company does well. However, should the company go out of business, the stock would become worthless, and you will lose all of your money. Should I diversify my investments?

Most financial advisors instruct their clients to diversify, which means investing in various areas. Instead of putting your money into only one stock, they suggest investing in multiple types of investments, including bonds, stocks, and mutual funds.

Chapter Six: How Can I Pay For College With Tax Savings?

What is a college savings plan?

In 1997 the US Government created the 529 Plan. It is named after a section in the IRS tax code, section 529. 529 Plans are designed to help families save for college by offering tax advantages to the money deposited in these types of accounts. Each state sponsors the plans, and each state has its own rules governing the use of the money. It offers additional benefits because each state can offer its perks and bonuses for people saving for college.

Here are just some of the benefits a 529 College Savings Plan can offer you:

No Federal Tax on Earnings

The 529 plan grows tax-free. That means no matter how much interest you earn over the life of the college savings plan, you will not have to pay taxes. It is perhaps the single most significant benefit of the 529 plan.

Better Earnings Than You Could Ever Get with a Savings Account

With 529s, you choose investments and compare the performance of different funds, which each carry a certain level of risk versus reward. You can change your choices once a year only, so it's a good idea to take the time to do the research to see which of the options has been consistently giving the best rate of return over the past five years.

These are mutual funds, that is, baskets of stocks. The types of stocks vary, so chances are a few may go down, and several may go up, evening out the rate of return. In a bad stock market, the portfolio's value might take a plunge, but on the other hand, you can buy low and make money as the market starts to improve.

State Tax Deductions

Because 529 plans are regulated and controlled by the state, the state tax deductions also vary. Some states also offer a tax deduction if you invest in a 529 plan.

Gift Tax Benefit

Usually, you can gift someone $15,000 per year without them having to pay taxes on the money (the gift allowance). While each state has upper limits, in most cases, you can add more than $15k to every 529 accounts and deduct it from your taxes.

Anyone Can Contribute

529 plans offer a liberal open participation plan. Anyone can contribute to a 529 plan. It means if you have friends, parents, or relatives who want to give gifts or help contribute, they can put money into the 529 plan as well, for even more savings. There are several ways to add to the account, including Upromise credit cards linked to the 529 accounts and more. Their direct contributions would also be tax-deductible depending on the state in which they lived.

Another important consideration is who the account holder will be. Parents can set up a 529, of course, but the money in that account would be factored into any financial aid package a college was to calculate for your child. If the account has been opened by a grandparent, aunt, uncle, and so on, it would not be considered.

No Age Limits

In most instances, it doesn't matter how old the recipient is. You can even save for your graduate school through a 529. So long as you spend the money on educational pursuits, such as paying tuition directly to the college, the funds will be tax-free.

Generally Low Fees

Many savings accounts charge such high fees it almost doesn't seem worth it. However, most 529 plans have fairly low fees and a low expense ratio. A low expense ratio means you save money on fees.

There are often no sales or commissions paid out for investing the money. You can only change your choices once a year, as we mentioned, but there are usually no fees when you make these changes.

Low Startup Enrollment Requirements

If you have ever looked into an interest-earning investment plan, you may have been shocked to see the enrollment requirements for starting investments. Most 529 plans have a very low threshold, in most cases as little as $25.

High Contribution Ceiling

Depending on the sponsoring state, you can contribute up to $520,000 in one account or across all accounts. That's still a significant amount of tax-free money for college. While you cannot contribute beyond your state's cap, you can continue to earn interest on the account beyond that limit.

In other words, you could superfund it and then let it sit there earning profits year after year. And of course, once you make a withdrawal from the account for educational purposes, such as $50,000 for the first year of college, you can always start contributing again, for example, because you want to start saving for grad school.

Complete Control

The account owner always has complete control of the assets in the account regardless of the beneficiary's age. You can also change the beneficiary.

That means if you dont go to college for any reason, you can transfer the account to a younger sibling, a niece, or nephew.

Alternatives To College Savings Plans

If you walk into the door of a financial advisor and ask them about college savings plans, they will recommend or discuss four options with you. We have already spent quite a few pages discussing one possibility – the 529 college savings plan.

This plan has many benefits. First and foremost is the tax savings, both Federal and state, that you can receive. It's also a very flexible option that can be adjusted and transferred as your needs change. The funds can be applied to any accredited institution – there are very few limitations. It can be used to pay for other educational costs outside of tuition, such as room and board, books, travel to and from college, and other expenses, often adding up to more than the tuition itself. It can even be used to pay back certain kinds of student loans.

The next option your financial advisor may discuss with you is called a Prepaid Tuition Plan.

Prepaid Tuition Plans

If you are certain you will be going to a state school, you may want to look into a prepaid tuition plan. These plans are set up so you can lock in college tuition at today's rates. For example, if you will be going to college in 10 years, you can lock in the tuition rate now for this year, and that's what you will pay ten years from now.

It saves you the cost of inflation and tuition hikes.

There are a few caveats here which need to be taken into consideration:

1-The school you are interested in has to participate in the plan. A prepaid tuition plan doesn't work for every college or university.

2-You can choose from a prepaid unit or a contract. With a contract, you commit to a predetermined number of years at that college, and the contract will often include room and board.

Prepaid units are just that: you purchase a fixed percentage of the tuition upfront, and the rest will be payable when they go to college. Regardless of which plan you choose, the purchase price will reflect your age, how many units you purchase, or how long a contract you are buying.

The rate you pay may also reflect how you fund the plan – lump sum versus instalment plans. The younger you are, the better rate you will receive because it provides the state with more time to invest and profit from your early payment.

3-The risks are that even with the preferential treatment, your child might not make the grade at the college or have higher aspirations and not want to attend that college. With the prepaid option, they might use up their tuition and then transfer to a more prestigious college (but also a more expensive one), leaving you with a shortfall of funds to pay for the rest of their education.

Education Savings Account (ESA).

This is the only education plan for college expenses and paying for private school for kindergarten through twelfth grade. Additionally, this plan allows contributions for special needs people of any age. It is less popular because the annual contribution is limited to $2,000, and you cannot change the beneficiary.

Education Savings Account Specifics:

- Interest from Education Savings Accounts grows income tax-free;
- Contributions are non-deductible for Federal income tax purposes;
- The contribution is a maximum of $2,000 per year per child under age eighteen, and there is no age limit for a special needs child;
- Funds can be used for kindergarten through high school, undergraduate, or graduate programs;
- Funds must be used only by the account beneficiary (who can be anyone), and there is no provision for changing the beneficiary;

Tips for Parents

Financial success comes about from a concerted effort starting from the early age when simple lessons are imparted. Parents have a big role to play and will contribute to the financial success of their childhood when they are finally adults. Parents can utilize the following tips:

Introduce the Idea of Money

Acquaint small children with coins first. Show them the estimation of coins and urge them to save their cash in a stash. Utilize a reasonable stash or container so that children can see their heap of money develop.

Give them genuine money to oversee - Nothing beats simple exercises. Start with basic activities and shopping trips. Make your children handle money and tally change. So they know-how – as well as so they look and feel confident doing it. A model: Christmas shopping for family members. Set the sum and perceive how they work it out. It is okay to make ideas, however, permit them to settle on decisions.

Talk about needs and wants

The initial phase in showing kids the benefit of saving is to assist them with separating wants and needs. Clarify that needs incorporate the essentials, like food, cover, fundamental dress, medical care, and instruction. For the most part, wages are the additional items—from film tickets and candy to planner shoes, a bike, or the most recent cell phone. You can utilize your budget, as an illustration, to delineate how wants should take a rearward sitting arrangement to needs as far as spending.

Let Them Bring in Their Own Money

If you need your kids to become savers, permit them to bring in and set aside money and give them the chance to figure out how to utilize it. At the point when you offer allowances in return for tasks, they're additionally learning the value of their diligent effort.

Have Them Track Spending

Part of being a superior saver implies knowing where your money is going. If your kids get a stipend, having them record their purchases every day and add them up toward the week's end can be an enlightening encounter. Urge them to consider how they're spending and how much quicker they could arrive at their reserve funds objective if they somehow managed to change their spending designs.

Set Savings Objectives

To a child, being advised to save—without clarifying why—may appear to be futile. Assisting kids to outline a saving objective can be a superior method to get them roused. If they understand what they need to put something aside for, help them separate their objectives into reasonable nibbles. On the off chance that they need to purchase a $50 computer game, for instance, and they get a $10 recompense every week, help them sort out how long it will take for them to arrive at that objective in light of their investment funds rate.

Give a place to Save

When your kids have a savings objective as a main priority, they'll need a spot to stash their money. This might be a stash for more youthful children, yet if they're somewhat more established, you might need to set them up with their checking or investment account at a bank. That way, they can perceive how their investment funds are adding up and how much advancement they're making toward their objective.

Offer Savings Motivations

One reason individuals save in their boss' retirement plan is the organization coordinating with commitment. Who doesn't care about the expectation of complimentary money? In case you're experiencing difficulty rousing your children to save, you can go through that equivalent rule to incline their endeavors. If your youngster has defined a significant investment fund objective—for instance, a $400 tablet—you could offer to coordinate with a level of what they have saved. As another option, you could offer an award when your child arrives at an investment funds achievement, for example, a $50 reward for hitting the midway imprint.

Leave Space for Errors

Some portion of placing kids in charge of their own money allows them to gain from their mistakes. It's enticing to step in and steer kids from a conceivably exorbitant mix-up. However, it very well might be wiser to utilize that botch as a teachable moment. That way, they'll know later on how not to manage their money.

Make Learning Fun

Play money games that support learning. Tabletop games, web-based games, and natively constructed games are generally potential outcomes.

Go about as Their Loan boss

One of the fundamental precepts of saving is not to maintain an unsustainable lifestyle. On the off chance that your youngster has something they need to purchase and is fretful about putting something aside for it, turning into your child's leaser can assist with showing a significant exercise saving. Say your youngster needs to buy something that costs $100.

You could loan them money and require installment from the stipend you give, with a premium. The exercise you need to instruct is that saving may mean deferring satisfaction longer, yet the thing you need to purchase will wind up costing less on the off chance you stand by.

Discussion about Money

On the off chance that you need children to find out about saving, it should be a continuous conversation. Regardless of whether you plan a customary week by week registration to discuss money or bring in money talks a piece of your day by day round, the key is to make a big difference for the discussion.

Set a Genuine Example

If you need your youngsters to become savers, being one yourself can help. Getting your secret stash fit as a fiddle, opening a bank account, or expanding your arrangement commitments are all means that you can require to support saving as a family movement. You could likewise choose to put something aside for something together, like an extra-large flat-screen television, a family get-away, or a pool.

Ways to increase your kids financial IQ

Of course, you have the simplicity of just having regular talks with your child, but to keep them interested and engaged in the world of finance, you must come up with creative ways to help them retain their knowledge. Studies have it that you must understand the practicality of it in real life for you to learn something truly.

It would be best if you made your child genuinely understand finance and financial responsibilities on an intellectual level. You should constantly think of creative ways to help your child enhance their financial IQ without having the added pressure of having to learn something they lack interest in.

Personal Finance is a frequently ignored topic in the American educational framework. With such a variety of Americans battling with money management issues, personal finance ought to be taught in our education systems at an early age. Since it is not, it is up to each person to ensure that they are legitimately schooled in the financial coliseum.

If we begin instructing ourselves about personal finance, can help correct this mistake and we start by teaching it to our kids.

Financial education is so critical. Money Crashers, is one of many websites that can help with the instruction of how to manage your money. You will get more information on educational assistance later in this chapter.

Here are five great routes for you to expand your financial IQ:

Books and magazines

Whether it's generally bound books or computerized substance, books and magazines are an extraordinary approach to growing your financial learning. Books like the "Aggregate Money Makeover" and the "Keen Investor" can instruct investors on everything from escaping debt to picking winning investment systems. For two or three dollars, you can learn handy tips and procedures that will improve your accounts and advantage you for whatever remains of your life.

You can likewise get tips from magazines like Kiplinger's on themes, for example, escaping debt and how to procure additional income. Perusing is an excellent approach to increment financial education for both grown-ups and children. In this way, make a beeline for your neighborhood Barnes and Noble or visit Amazon.com and begin perusing!

Courses

Go to a neighborhood fund class. There are a vast amount of free financial courses that offer a scope of accommodating insights.

You can discover these at your neighborhood bank or credit union. Additional workshops at stadiums and tradition focus on huge name speakers like Suze Orman or Dave Ramsey.

You might be motivated by seeing one of these personal fund masters talk in person about every day financial issues. These classes make cost money! Make sure to avoid a portion of the deceitful "free" advancements at these workshops; organizations at times will utilize high weight deal systems to drive you into purchasing costly organization items.

Online websites

Would you like to learn about personal money for free? At that point, make sure to check out online individual account sites and websites. Locales like:

* Free Money Finance
* MoneyNing
* Wise Bread

These are incredible online assets to begin. I might be reasonably one-sided; however, Money Crashers is an excellent site to start learning the nuts and bolts also! There is a considerable amount of helpful money-saving tips and audits of financial items.

Additionally, investigate money gatherings in which you can increase important information from different clients. What are you sitting tight for? Begin googling!

TV programs

While financial TV programs alone won't make you financially capable, they can be significant learning devices. You can learn a considerable amount from the life lessons of other people.

I proposed that TV watchers check out Dave Ramsey, Suze Orman, and Jim Cramer.

Smartphone Applications

It might appear to be incredible, yet your smart telephone can help you with your money.
Top Budget and tracker management apps:

Mint

https://mint.intuit.com/

Personal Capital

https://www.personalcapital.com/

YNAB

https://www.youneedabudget.com/

Countabout

https://countabout.com/

Financial Terminology For Beginners

- Check: this is a piece of paper that the bank will give to you. You will put in the amount you would like to pay from your checking account and the person to whom the money should go.

- Credit: this is a trust that will allow the one party, or the lender, to provide resources or money to another party or the borrower. If the borrower honors the contract and repays the money on time or by agreement, they will receive excellent credit. They will have a higher chance to borrow money again later on at a lower interest rate, saving themselves some money in the process.

- Interest: this is the payment given by the borrower to the lender for the borrowed money. It is like a fee for the borrowed money.

- Dividend: This is a quarterly, bi-annually, or yearly payment made by a corporation to the shareholders as a reward for investing in the company. It is usually given as the profits or the distributions of the company.

- Mutual fund: an investment enterprise is going to operate it. It is a fared investment fund that will collect its money from many different investors and then use it to purchase stocks and securities.

- Savings: money that has been accumulated and set aside.

- Savings account: this is an account that a credit union or a bank usually maintains. It is going to pay a small amount of interest on the money that you deposit inside.

- Stock: when you purchase a stock in a company, you will own some businesses that provide security. As the owner, you will have the right to receive this dividend or a part of the profits based on how many stocks you own. But if the company doesn't earn money or loses money, you will not earn anything, and the value of your stock will go down.

- Compound interest: is known as interest paid on both the principal and interest typically received in a bank account and can be paid daily, monthly, quarterly, semiannually, or annually.

- Tax: The portion of your income paid to the Government for things such as your police and fire services, streets, bus systems, etc. Taxes may be charged on most types of income, on sale of assets, on most types of purchases, and even on the value of what people own when they die.

- Profit: The amount left over from a product or service sale after deducting all expenses related to that product or service.

- Asset: something that puts money in your pocket

Conclusion

Congratulations! You have made it. You have reached the end of this book, but honestly, it is only the start of a most magnificent journey!

In a world where free things are rare, money is an important concept to learn and understand. However, it is not enough to learn just about money. To succeed in life and one's financial goals, it is crucial to learn every aspect of it, from saving to investing.

Children must have money because it is a part of life. We live in a world that uses the money to function. Money is used to build schools, pay teachers, print school books, tailor school uniforms, pay for transportation, purchase cars, drive to take children to school, pick them up after school, buy food, and so on.

It is also crucial for children to have money to learn the value or worth of cash. When this learning begins, they can distinguish the denominations of currencies, their worth against products and services in their respective countries and other countries in the world. For example, a child may have money from one country and travel to another country to believe that the currency will be accepted there. The child will then conduct a transaction and then understand the currency has no worth in that country.It can sadden a child and raise many questions that frequently remain un-answered.

Another reason is not to become vulnerable to money. When children do not have money and are attracted to something to the point they must have it, actions are taken.

Some adults find themselves buried in debt and with a high negative net worth. While this results from their personal choices, their parents bear some blame for what they have become. Parents, as the primary educators of children, are responsible for teaching the basic concepts of money.

By teaching personal finance to your child, you give him more chances of succeeding and achieving his financial goals in life. Teaching personal finance is crucial to your child's growth, as it is not included in most schools but considered necessary in life.

However, this should be done considering the child's age, readiness, and maturity level.

School is important. You get an education from it to earn a degree, but you need more than that to get ahead in life. Money is an essential tool. By teaching your kids about it, you are helping them get that step ahead.

The next step is to take action. A person who does not read is not much better than a person who cannot read. Faith without works is dead. Likewise, information without action is futile. You cannot manage your money only by reading about it and feeling good. You have to take action and use your personal power to make it work for you!

Thank You

I want to thank you for the purchase of this book and more importantly, I want to thank you for reading it. I trust that the information inside helped to increase your knowledge about basic personal finance. Giving your children this foundational information can help them manage money for the rest of their life. An amazing gift.

Finally, if you enjoyed this book, please leave a review for this book on Amazon.com. That action helps out a great deal and is much appreciated!

Warm Regards,
Thomas Turner

https://www.amazon.com/dp/B093MQL61S
ASIN: B093MQL61S

Customer reviews

4.6 out of 5 stars   4.6 out of 5
                        6 global ratings

| 5 star | 64% |
| 4 star | 36% |

3 star 0% (0%)   0%
2 star 0% (0%)   0%
1 star 0% (0%)

Review this product

Share your thoughts with other customers

(Write a Customer Review)

Made in the USA
Las Vegas, NV
04 August 2024

93345515R00057